MW01702853

E

SRA

Specific Skill Series

for Language Arts

Mechanics

Leveled Books in Nine Key Language Arts Skill Areas

SRA

Columbus, OH

The McGraw·Hill Companies

Cover: ©PhotoDisc/Getty Images, Inc.

SRAonline.com

SRA

Copyright © 2005 by SRA/McGraw-Hill.

All rights reserved. Except as permitted under the United States Copyright Act, no part of this publication may be reproduced or distributed in any form or by any means, or stored in a database or retrieval system, without the prior written permission of the publisher, unless otherwise indicated.

Send all inquiries to:
SRA/McGraw-Hill
8787 Orion Place
Columbus, OH 43240-4027

Printed in the United States of America.

ISBN 0-07-601703-6

3 4 5 6 7 8 9 10 GLO 15 14 13 12 11

GENERAL INFORMATION ON MECHANICS

Mechanics involves the conventions of punctuation and capitalization. The purpose of punctuation is to show how language is divided into sentences and sentence parts and how those parts are related. Punctuation marks make writing easier to read and the meaning of written language clearer. In speech, students can produce sentences as easily as they can walk, but in writing they must think about what a sentence is and follow the rules of mechanics in order to effectively communicate.

Knowledge of proper punctuation and capitalization is vitally important in the proofreading phase of the writing process. Research shows that the best way to teach English-language conventions is in the context of their importance in the editing and proofreading phases of the writing process. Students should be taught that correcting errors in capitalization and punctuation is an editorial skill rather than a composing skill.

ABOUT *SPECIFIC SKILL SERIES FOR LANGUAGE ARTS*

Specific Skill Series for Language Arts is a companion to ***Specific Skill Series,*** a supplemental reading program that has been widely recognized for its effectiveness for over thirty years. The two series are designed and organized the same. ***Specific Skill Series for Language Arts*** consists of discrete units of practice exercises that target and reinforce fundamental language-arts skills. Units in both series are presented in multiple-choice format for standardized test practice.

ABOUT *MECHANICS*

The scope and sequence for Books A through H of *Mechanics* focuses on the conventions of punctuation and capitalization. The scope and sequence for each book is located on the last page of the book. Each unit includes

- **rule boxes** that explain mechanics rules.
- **models** in each rule box to illustrate the language point being discussed.
- **multiple-choice exercises** for skills practice and reinforcement.

Four **Language Activity Pages** (LAPs) appear in each book. Each LAP is divided into the following four sections and reviews the skills practiced in the preceding units:

Exercising Your Skill reviews key terms and concepts.
Expanding Your Skill provides mixed practice.
Exploring Language shows how the skills apply to real-world contexts by featuring one of six forms of writing: descriptive, narrative, personal, persuasive, expository, and poetry.
Expressing Yourself includes two creative activities related to the skills. One activity is always a Work-with-a-Partner activity to encourage collaborative learning.

TO THE TEACHER

SERIES COMPONENTS

- **Student Editions:** Nine books in each level (A–H) focus on nine skill areas: *Grammar, Usage, Mechanics, Spelling, Vocabulary, Sentences, Paragraphs, Writing Process,* and *Research.*
- **Placement Test Books:** One book for each skill area includes diagnostic tests to place students in the correct level.
- **Teacher's Manual:** Primarily an answer key, the *Teacher's Manual* also includes reproducible student worksheets and further information on how to use the program, including classroom management tips.

HOW TO USE *SPECIFIC SKILL SERIES FOR LANGUAGE ARTS*

Placing Students in Levels: The scope and sequence, complexity of skills, and readability in Levels A through H correspond to Grades 1 through 8. Students may, however, be placed in any level. For example, in the second grade, a student who needs remedial work in a specific skill may be placed in Book A, an on-level student who would benefit from skills reinforcement may be placed in Book B, and an advanced student who is ready for enrichment may be placed in Book C or higher. *Placement Tests* help place students in the correct level.

Setting: This series can be used for independent study and one-on-one practice sessions, as well as in small-group and whole-class settings. It is also effective in after-school and summer-school programs.

Getting Started: Students must have notebook paper or copies of reproducible student worksheets (located in the *Teacher's Manual*) before they begin working. Remind students not to write in the books. Students may begin in any unit of any book, depending on the skill practice they need, although it is recommended that they begin with Unit 1. As they work through the units, students should record their answers on notebook paper or on the student worksheets.

Pacing: Students should be encouraged to work at their own pace, completing a few units every day or every other day.

Scoring: Teachers should score units as soon as they have been completed. Then a discussion can be held in which students justify their answer choices.

Internet Use: Some activities, especially those in *Research,* require students to use the Internet. Students' use of the Internet should be monitored closely for content appropriateness and safety.

TO THE STUDENT

Mechanics are the rules for capitalization and punctuation. Following these rules will make your writing clear and correct.

In Book E *Mechanics,* you will learn about

- Capitalization
- End Marks
- Abbreviations
- Commas
- Colons, Semicolons, and Hyphens
- Quotation Marks and Underlining
- Dashes
- Parentheses
- Ellipses Points
- Apostrophes

After you complete this book, you will be able to properly use semicolons. A semicolon can be used to link two independent clauses.

> Baton Rouge is the capital of Louisiana**;** *baton rouge* means "red stick" in French.

You will also learn the purposes of other punctuation marks, including dashes, parentheses, ellipses points, and apostrophes.

> Long Dash: In 1682 René-Robert Cavelier**—**he was a trader**—** rediscovered the area now known as Louisiana.
>
> Parentheses and Short Dash: Hernando de Soto **(**c.1496**-**1542**)** was one of the first Europeans to explore the region.
>
> Ellipses Points: Archibald MacLeish wrote, "Summer is drawn blinds in Louisiana **. . .** shade of elms and maples in New England."
>
> Apostrophe: Louisiana**'**s state insect is the honeybee.

By mastering the skills in this book, you will be able to capitalize and punctuate your writing correctly.

Unit 1
Capitalization

There are many rules for using **capital letters.**

- A sentence always begins with a capital letter.
  Lightning streaks across the sky.
- The pronoun *I* is always a capital letter.
  When **I** heard the thunderstorm, **I** looked out my window.
- A person's name, initials, and title start with capital letters.
  Miss **J**ennifer **C**. **T**hompson **S**ergeant **E**mmanuel **J**. **V**asquez
- Pet names and words used as names begin with capital letters.
  Felix the dog **A**unt **K**im **D**ad (but *my dad*, not *my Dad*)
- A speaker's or a quotation's first word begins with a capital letter.
  "**A**m I the only person who heard that?" asked Connie.
  Grandma always said, "**P**atience is half the struggle."

In which part of each sentence is there a capitalization error? If there is not an error, choose *None*.

1. My first visit (A) | to San Francisco was (B) | when i was sixteen. (C) | None (D)

2. Brooke told (A) | grandma about (B) | summer camp. (C) | None (D)

3. The old saying (A) | is, "a captain goes (B) | down with his ship." (C) | None (D)

4. my brother (A) | asked, "Should I pack (B) | your lunch too?" (C) | None (D)

5. Our dog chopper (A) | plays with a tennis ball (B) | for hours each day. (C) | None (D)

6. The time (A) | on that clock (B) | is wrong. (C) | None (D)

7. As we jogged (A) | up the street, we saw (B) | Uncle tony in his new car. (C) | None (D)

8.	Is the name	Steven c. Berg	or Steven T. Berg?	None
	(A)	(B)	(C)	(D)
9.	next week	we will begin	our state history reports.	None
	(A)	(B)	(C)	(D)
10.	Vic asked	general O'Neil about	his training assignment.	None
	(A)	(B)	(C)	(D)
11.	Since his return,	I have not seen	Mr. murphy.	None
	(A)	(B)	(C)	(D)
12.	We think our art teacher,	Mrs. Lombardo,	is the best.	None
	(A)	(B)	(C)	(D)
13.	What does the	saying "a stitch in time	saves nine" mean?	None
	(A)	(B)	(C)	(D)
14.	The sweater i	knitted does	not look even.	None
	(A)	(B)	(C)	(D)
15.	"Can you hear	the cheers from	the arena?" asked Rob.	None
	(A)	(B)	(C)	(D)
16.	Grandma adopted	a cat and	named her flash.	None
	(A)	(B)	(C)	(D)
17.	where is	the index for	this encyclopedia set?	None
	(A)	(B)	(C)	(D)
18.	The nameplate	on this door	reads dr. Priscilla Markson.	None
	(A)	(B)	(C)	(D)
19.	My dad and I	rode a bicycle built for two	on Saturday.	None
	(A)	(B)	(C)	(D)

Unit 1
Capitalization

- Holiday names always begin with a capital letter.
  Independence Day
- The name of a language, a religion, or a nationality begins with a capital letter.
  Swedish **Hinduism** **Swiss**
- In titles, first, last, and other main words begin with a capital letter. When they are not first or last in a title, words such as *a, an, and, as, at, by, for, in, of, on, or, the,* and *to* do not begin with a capital letter. Titles of songs, poems, short stories, art, and newspapers also follow this rule.
  Book title: ***Pearls of the Sea***
  Magazine title: ***Nature's Way***
  Film or movie title: ***On the Road Again***
- An important document or award name begins with a capital letter.
  Bill of Rights **Nobel Peace Prize**
- The names of particular buildings, bridges, monuments, and other structures begin with a capital letter.
  Sears Tower **Brooklyn Bridge** **Lincoln Memorial** **Jacobs Field**

In which part of each sentence is there a capitalization error? If there is not an error, choose *None*.

20. Did you know (A) | that Keith's family (B) | is scottish? (C) | None (D)

21. The medal of honor (A) | is the highest award (B) | for courage. (C) | None (D)

22. He is reading (A) | *the Autobiography* (B) | *of Benjamin Franklin.* (C) | None (D)

23. What is (A) | the date of (B) | labor Day this year? (C) | None (D)

24. Levi Carr's article (A) | is in this month's (B) | issue of *Cobblestone*. (C) | None (D)

Unit 1
Capitalization

25.	I hope I can stay up **(A)**	until midnight **(B)**	on new year's eve. **(C)**	None **(D)**
26.	The space needle **(A)**	in Seattle is a **(B)**	popular tourist attraction. **(C)**	None **(D)**
27.	The Pentagon is one **(A)**	of this country's **(B)**	largest office buildings. **(C)**	None **(D)**
28.	This week's **(A)**	read-aloud book **(B)**	is *A walk in the woods.* **(C)**	None **(D)**
29.	Mom remembers **(A)**	hearing her grandparents **(B)**	speak russian. **(C)**	None **(D)**
30.	Tickets for the movie **(A)**	*Time stands Still* **(B)**	are sold out. **(C)**	None **(D)**
31.	The origins of buddhism **(A)**	can be traced **(B)**	to India. **(C)**	None **(D)**
32.	The audience applauded **(A)**	for the actor's **(B)**	first emmy Award. **(C)**	None **(D)**
33.	The poem **(A)**	"One Snowflake" **(B)**	is brief and simple. **(C)**	None **(D)**
34.	Is a copy of **(A)**	the declaration of independence **(B)**	in this museum? **(C)**	None **(D)**
35.	One of my family's **(A)**	thanksgiving traditions **(B)**	is to volunteer. **(C)**	None **(D)**
36.	The golden gate bridge **(A)**	is about sixty miles **(B)**	from here. **(C)**	None **(D)**

Unit 1
Capitalization

- Product names begin with a capital letter.
  Jumps shoes   **B**itty **B**ites birdseed
- Business, group, or organization names begin with a capital letter.
  The **B**argain **B**asement   **F**un-**F**or-**A**ll **F**itness
- Abbreviations that use the first letter of each word in a name use capital letters.
  ADA ⟶ American Dental Association
  USPS ⟶ United States Postal Service
- School subjects that refer to a language or include a number begin with a capital letter.
  Latin   **A**lgebra 2

Which item corrects the capitalization error from each sentence?

37. The Wells School Foundation, or wsf, has a fund-raiser tomorrow.
(A) Wells school foundation
(B) WSF
(C) Fund-raiser

38. Please buy hair-glo instead of that new brand of shampoo we tried.
(A) Shampoo
(B) Hair-Glo
(C) Brand

39. I would like to study greek, but it is not offered until next term.
(A) Greek
(B) Next Term
(C) But

40. The american animal alliance hosts weekly meetings in that school.
(A) School
(B) Weekly
(C) American Animal Alliance

41. This store sells jeans I like, including genie and Denwear brands.
(A) Store
(B) Jeans
(C) Genie

42. The city ballet company will perform in our auditorium today.
(A) City Ballet Company
(B) Our
(C) Auditorium

43. The uaw represents workers in the automotive industry.
(A) Automotive
(B) Workers
(C) UAW

44. The united states olympic committee plans events years in advance.
(A) Events
(B) United States Olympic Committee
(C) In Advance

45. Aunt Lynn used finer Shine to wax her car.
(A) Finer
(B) Wax
(C) Car

46. Our school's pto meets every other Thursday at 7:00 P.M.
(A) PTO
(B) Other
(C) School's

47. I wonder if it is easy or difficult to write words in japanese.
(A) Words
(B) Japanese
(C) If

48. The national library association has a book auction every year.
(A) Every Year
(B) Auction
(C) National Library Association

Unit 2
Capitalization

- The name of a city, a county, a state, a country, or a continent begins with a capital letter.
  Jacksonville **L**ake **C**ounty **M**aryland **I**taly **A**ustralia
- Bodies of water and geographical places begin with a capital letter.
  Gulf of **M**exico **P**ike's **P**eak **S**equoia **N**ational **F**orest
- Direction words start with a capital letter only when they refer to specific sections of the country.
  Driving to the **E**ast **C**oast from the **W**est, we saw many mountains.
  Is **I**nterstate 70 north or south of here?
- The name of a special event begins with a capital letter.
  Founder's **D**ay **P**arade **W**orld **S**eries
- The name of a historical period begins with a capital letter.
  Middle **A**ges **G**reat **D**epression

Around the Country

In which part of each sentence is there a capitalization error? If there is not an error, choose *None*.

1.	In oxford county,	Elephant Mountain	is 3,744 feet.	None
	(A)	(B)	(C)	(D)

2.	The primary river	in New Hampshire	is the merrimack river.	None
	(A)	(B)	(C)	(D)

3.	To learn about	the colonial period,	visit Williamsburg.	None
	(A)	(B)	(C)	(D)

4.	In the south,	there are many sites	that recall the Civil War.	None
	(A)	(B)	(C)	(D)

5.	Gilbert, South Carolina,	hosts a Peach Festival	every July.	None
	(A)	(B)	(C)	(D)

6.	Circleville, ohio,	is home to a Pumpkin Show	every October.	None
	(A)	(B)	(C)	(D)

7.	In Washington state,	colville national forest	is lush.	None
	(A)	(B)	(C)	(D)

8. Tennessee is | directly west | of north carolina. None
(A) (B) (C) (D)

9. Boonville, Missouri, | is the site of | the big muddy folk festival. None
(A) (B) (C) (D)

10. As the west grew, | thousands of people | went through Missouri. None
(A) (B) (C) (D)

11. Rosebud, | South Dakota, is | in Todd County. None
(A) (B) (C) (D)

12. The city of rosebud | has an important history | of Sioux tribes. None
(A) (B) (C) (D)

13. Dinosaur national Monument | spans Colorado | and Utah. None
(A) (B) (C) (D)

14. Wizard Island | is in the middle of | crater lake in Oregon. None
(A) (B) (C) (D)

15. There is | a royal palace | in Oahu, Hawaii. None
(A) (B) (C) (D)

16. Hawaii, | located in the pacific ocean, | used to have monarchs. None
(A) (B) (C) (D)

17. Iolani Palace in Hawaii | is america's | only palace. None
(A) (B) (C) (D)

18. The gold rush | started in California | late in the 1840s. None
(A) (B) (C) (D)

19. In 1846, | the battle at palo alto | began the Mexican War. None
(A) (B) (C) (D)

Unit 2
Capitalization

- The name of a day or a month begins with a capital letter.
  Thursday **F**ebruary
- Each word in the greeting of a letter begins with a capital letter.
  Dear **C**athy,
- Only the first word in the closing of a letter begins with a capital letter.
  Your friend,
- Capital letters are used in an outline to label supporting ideas.
  I. School lunches (In this case, *I* is a Roman numeral.)
  A. High in starch
  B. Often over-cooked

Read each letter. Look carefully at the underlined parts. Is each underlined part capitalized correctly? If it is, choose *Correct*. If it is *not* correct, choose the answer that shows correct capitalization.

(20) Tuesday, August 16, 2005

(21) dear Ben,

There are only three more weeks until school starts! What did you do this summer? I went on a vacation with my family that started on (22) Saturday, july 30. In Arkansas, we traveled to Hot Springs. It is sort of weird to see warm water bubble out of the ground. We had fun!

(23) See You Soon,

Tim

20. (A) tuesday, August 16, 2005
(B) Tuesday, august 16, 2005
(C) tuesday, august 16, 2005
(D) Correct

21. (A) Dear Ben,
(B) dear ben,
(C) Dear ben,
(D) Correct

22. **(A)** saturday, july 30
(B) saturday, July 30
(C) Saturday, July 30
(D) Correct

---

23. **(A)** See you Soon,
(B) See you soon,
(C) see you soon,
(D) Correct

(24) saturday, december 3, 2005

Dear Mrs. Marcum,

Here is the outline for my physical fitness report. Please read it, and let me know what you think.

I. Skateboarding advantages
  A. Fresh air
  B. Good exercise

II. Skateboarding disadvantages

(25) a. Possible injuries
  b. Property damage

Sincerely,

Alicia

24. **(A)** Saturday, december 3, 2005
(B) saturday, December 3, 2005
(C) Saturday, December 3, 2005
(D) Correct

---

25. **(A)** A. Possible injuries
  B. Property damage
(B) A. Possible injuries
  b. Property damage
(C) a. Possible injuries
  B. Property damage
(D) Correct

Unit 3
End Marks

Different types of sentences require different end marks.

- A sentence that tells or commands ends with a **period** (.).
    The telephone is ringing. Please answer the telephone.
- A sentence that asks something ends with a **question mark** (?).
    Who called on the telephone?
- A sentence that shows strong feeling ends with an **exclamation point** (!).
    Grandma is on the telephone!
- In direct speech, an end mark goes inside the quotation marks (“ ”).
    Chloe said to Grandma, “When can you visit us?”

The Last Day of School

Is the end mark in each sentence correct?

1. Mr. Milne said excitedly, “The last day of school is just days away”!
(A) Yes **(B)** No

2. Mr. Milne explained that the fifth-grade class is allowed to plan its own end-of-the-school year party.
(A) Yes **(B)** No

3. Judy asked, “What are our choices for the party?”
(A) Yes **(B)** No

4. “Your choices are up to all the fifth-graders,” smiled the teacher.
(A) Yes **(B)** No

5. Dominic asked, “Does that mean we can choose anything”?
(A) Yes **(B)** No

6. Mr. Milne told him that student ideas would have to be within reason.
(A) Yes **(B)** No

7. “Come up with some ideas during lunch,” Mr. Milne said!
(A) Yes **(B)** No

8. Most of the fifth-graders shared their party ideas while eating lunch?
(A) Yes **(B)** No

9. Abby suggested having a picnic outside on the soccer field.
(A) Yes **(B)** No

10. Nick said, "I think we should have music?"
(A) Yes **(B)** No

11. One group of fifth-graders was chosen to list games to play?
(A) Yes **(B)** No

12. After lunch, students returned with many ideas for teachers to hear.
(A) Yes **(B)** No

13. All fifth-grade teachers will take the top two ideas from their classes to share with one another.
(A) Yes **(B)** No

14. Mr. Milne said, "This way each fifth-grader's input is considered".
(A) Yes **(B)** No

15. Mr. Milne asked for a volunteer to write party ideas on the board?
(A) Yes **(B)** No

16. With much enthusiasm, Josie quickly answered, "I will, I will!"
(A) Yes **(B)** No

17. Mr. Milne added one more idea to the list on the board.
(A) Yes **(B)** No

18. The class read the idea as he wrote it, and they could not believe it?
(A) Yes **(B)** No

19. Mr. Milne exclaimed, "A hot-air balloon will land on the field to kick off the fifth-grade party!"
(A) Yes **(B)** No

20. Then he added, "Don't worry, we will also use some of the party ideas from the fifth-grade students".
(A) Yes **(B)** No

The First LAP
Language Activity Pages

A. Exercising Your Skill

You have been learning about some of the rules for capitalizing letters, such as months, titles, and countries. You have also reviewed when to use a certain end mark. Number your paper from 1 to 10. Read the sentences below. Use a word from the box only once to complete each sentence correctly.

question	title	pronoun	feeling	Names
sentence	period	Direction	inside	first

1. A _____ always begins with a capital letter.
2. A quotation's _____ word begins with a capital letter.
3. _____ words do not always start with a capital letter.
4. The _____ *I* is always written as a capital letter.
5. _____ of languages begin with a capital letter.
6. There are some words in a _____ that may not be capitalized.
7. In direct speech, write an end mark _____ the quotation marks.
8. A _____ ends with a question mark.
9. A _____ is used at the end of a sentence that tells or commands.
10. Strong _____ in a sentence is shown with an exclamation point.

B. Expanding Your Skill

Number your paper from 1 to 8. Read the paragraph below. In each sentence, find the capitalization error. Some errors may be words that are improperly capitalized. Remember that the names of people, particular places, and special events begin with capital letters. Fix the errors, and write them correctly on your paper.

(1) Where can baseball fans train with Professional players? (2) This can happen at Fantasy baseball Camp. (3) Many major league teams sponsor such Camps. (4) Anyone over the age of thirty who can afford the fee can attend fantasy Baseball Camp. (5) Current and former Baseball players participate in these camps. (6) Not every baseball player can take part, but those who do show campers a glimpse of major League baseball skills. (7) Retired players, including Jim Palmer and brooks Robinson, enjoy helping fans understand why they still love the game. (8) Some camps are conducted in florida.

C. Exploring Language

Persuasive Writing Number your paper from 1 to 10. Read the selection below. It is an advertisement for a fantasy camp. Each numbered part has a capitalization or an end mark error. Find the errors. Then write the word correctly, or write the correct end mark on your paper.

(1) Fantasy hockey Camp

(2) Do you ever wonder what some hockey players do in the off-season! (3) The national Hockey League, or NHL, invites hockey fans to find out. (4) players of yesterday and today share some of their secrets about this great sport. (5) However, there are rules (6) Fans under the age of eighteen must have an adult attend Fantasy Hockey camp with them. (7) For safety reasons, "fans under the age of nine are not allowed to attend." (8) There are different fees depending on the length of time spent at camp? (9) So, pack your pads, pucks, and sticks for a great nhl adventure. (10) We are excited to see you there

D. Expressing Yourself

Choose one of these activities. When you are finished, give your paper to your teacher.

1. Think of a fantasy camp you would like to attend. Pretend that you have been there. Draw a color picture of something you did at fantasy camp. Write one sentence below your drawing to describe it. Make sure you use capital letters and end marks correctly. Now write a note to a friend or a family member that shares when you went to fantasy camp, where it was, and what your favorite thing about it was.

2. WORK with a PARTNER With a partner, write five questions you would ask a professional athlete of your choice. After the questions are written, one of you will pretend to be that athlete. The other person will pretend to be a reporter. The reporter chooses only three questions to ask. As the reporter asks the questions, the athlete writes his or her answers. Remember that direct speech uses quotation marks. Make sure end marks are correct with or without quotation marks.

Unit 4
Abbreviations

An **abbreviation** is a short way to write a word or a phrase. Some abbreviations are written with periods.

Doctor → Dr.

- The abbreviation of a person's title is followed by a period.

  Mr. Shaw   Mrs. Crane

- Each initial of a person's name is followed by a period.

  J. N. Ashman   Monica L. Schultz

- Time and ancient date abbreviations are followed by periods.

  6:25 A.M.   1:40 P.M.   13 B.C.   A.D. 527

- The abbreviation for a day of the week or the name of a month is followed by a period. Use these abbreviations in charts and lists only. However, *May, June,* and *July* are not abbreviated.

  Sun. Mon. Tues. Wed. Thurs. Fri. Sat.

  Jan. Feb. Mar. Apr. Aug. Sept. Oct. Nov. Dec.

- If a sentence ends with a period and its last word is an abbreviation, do not add another period. For example, *His name is Fred Gleason Jr.*

Which abbreviation is written correctly?

1. **(A)** Dr. O. Y. Nolan   **(B)** Dr. O Y. Nolan   **(C)** Dr. O Y Nolan
2. **(A)** Elaine D Adams   **(B)** Elaine. D. Adams   **(C)** Elaine D. Adams
3. **(A)** 9:07 PM   **(B)** 9:07 P.M.   **(C)** 9:07 PM.
4. **(A)** Se.pt. 26   **(B)** Sept 26   **(C)** Sept. 26
5. **(A)** S. Frank, D.D.S.   **(B)** S. Frank, DDS   **(C)** S. Frank, D.D.S
6. **(A)** Feb 3   **(B)** Feb. 3   **(C)** Feb 3.
7. **(A)** AD 409   **(B)** A.D. 409   **(C)** A.D 409
8. **(A)** Wed, May 11   **(B)** Wed., May 11   **(C)** WED., May. 11
9. **(A)** 52 B.C.   **(B)** 52 BC   **(C)** 52 B.C.
10. **(A)** 7:38 AM.   **(B)** 7:38 AM   **(C)** 7:38 A.M.

Unit 4
Abbreviations

- The abbreviation of the name of a street, a road, or a highway is followed by a period. Use these abbreviations only on envelopes.

street	St.	boulevard	Blvd.
road	Rd.	avenue	Ave.
court	Ct.	lane	Ln.
place	Pl.	drive	Dr.
route	Rte.	highway	Hwy.

Which abbreviation is written correctly?

11. **(A)** 614 Hwy 101
(B) 614 Hwy. 101

12. **(A)** 29401 Lakeshore Blvd.
(B) 29401 Lakeshore Blvrd.

13. **(A)** 875 Meadow Ln.
(B) 875 Meadow L.n.

14. **(A)** 23 Jordan Ct
(B) 23 Jordan Ct.

15. **(A)** 1867 Lloyd Rd.
(B) 1867 Lloyd .Rd

16. **(A)** 9800 Breckinridge .Dr.
(B) 9800 Breckinridge Dr.

17. **(A)** 5276 Rte. 43
(B) 5276 Rt. 43

18. **(A)** 1959 Wright Ave.
(B) 1959 Wright Avn.

19. **(A)** 350 Chevy Pl.
(B) 350 Chevy P.l.

20. **(A)** 48 Barnes Str.
(B) 48 Barnes St.

Unit 4
Abbreviations

- Here are examples of abbreviations that are not written with periods.

  eastern standard time ⟶ EST

  revolutions per minute ⟶ rpm

  frequency modulation ⟶ FM

  southwest ⟶ SW

- Two-letter post office abbreviations of a state's name do not include periods. Use these abbreviations only on envelopes. Check a dictionary if you do not know the abbreviation of a particular state.

Georgia	GA	South Dakota	SD
Alaska	AK	New Hampshire	NH

- Some abbreviations use the first letter of each word in a name. This type of abbreviation uses capital letters without periods.

  most valuable player ⟶ MVP

  Environmental Protection Agency ⟶ EPA

  digital video disc ⟶ DVD

Which underlined abbreviation is written correctly?

21. **(A)** Tallahassee, FL
(B) Tallahassee, FLA

22. **(A)** Lubbock, TEX
(B) Lubbock, TX

23. **(A)** Does the nfl have a headquarters?
(B) Does the NFL have a headquarters?

24. **(A)** That clock shows MST, or mountain standard time.
(B) That clock shows Mst, or mountain standard time.

25. **(A)** Santa Barbara, CALI
(B) Santa Barbara, CA

26. **(A)** My television has a V.C.R. built into it.
(B) My television has a VCR built into it.

27. **(A)** Providence, RI
(B) Providence, RI.

Unit 4

Abbreviations

In science reports, abbreviations for different units of measure are used.

- An abbreviation for an English unit of measure is followed by a period. The abbreviations are the same for singular and plural units *except* when they refer to time.

inch(es) = in.	foot (or feet) = ft.	yard(s) = yd.	mile(s) = mi.
cup(s) = c.	ounce(s) = oz.	gallon(s) = gal.	pound(s) = lb.

Time:	second = sec.	seconds = secs.
	minute = min.	minutes = mins.
	hour = hr.	hours = hrs.

- An abbreviation for a metric unit of measure is *not* followed by a period. The abbreviations are the same for singular and plural units.

kilometer(s) = km	meter(s) = m	centimeter(s) = cm
millimeter(s) = mm	kiloliter(s) = kL	liter(s) = L
milliliter(s) = mL	gram(s) = g	milligram(s) = mg

Which abbreviation is written correctly?

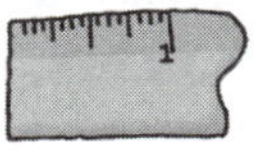

28. **(A)** 70 yds. **(B)** 70 yd **(C)** 70 yd.

29. **(A)** 2 c. **(B)** 2 cs. **(C)** 2 cp

30. **(A)** 3 m. **(B)** 3 mt **(C)** 3 m

31. **(A)** 14 secs **(B)** 14 secs. **(C)** 14 sec.

32. **(A)** 5 g **(B)** 5 gs **(C)** 5 g.

33. **(A)** 82 lbs. **(B)** 82 lb. **(C)** 82 lb

34. **(A)** 9 L. **(B)** 9 L **(C)** 9 Ls

35. **(A)** 6 gal. **(B)** 6 gals. **(C)** 6 gal

36. **(A)** 3,700 mis. **(B)** 3,700 mi **(C)** 3,700 mi.

37. **(A)** 4 km **(B)** 4 km. **(C)** 4 kms

38. **(A)** 1 hrs. **(B)** 1 hr **(C)** 1 hr.

Unit 5
Commas

A **comma** (,) is used to separate certain items in writing.

- In dates, use a comma between the day and month and the date and year.

  Saturday**,** March 19 March 19**,** 2005

However, never use a comma between the month and date or year.

March 19 *not* March, 19 March 2005 *not* March, 2005

In a sentence, follow the rules above for using commas. In a sentence with a complete date, add a comma after the last part of the date.

On Saturday**,** March 19**,** 2005**,** the event will begin.

- In addresses, use a comma between the city and state but *not* the state and ZIP code.

  Appleton**,** Wisconsin 54911

In a sentence, use a comma between the street and the city also. Add another comma after the last part of a complete address.

The store at 216 Cedar Avenue**,** Cleveland**,** Ohio 44113**,** is new.

If just a city and a state are in a sentence, add a comma after each one.

Helena**,** Montana**,** is the state's capital.

- In friendly letters, use a comma after the greeting. In all letters, use a comma after the closing.

  Dear Wanda**,** Sincerely**,**

Are commas used correctly?

1. Ypsilanti, Michigan
   (A) Yes **(B)** No

2. The publisher has an office in, Indianapolis Indiana.
   (A) Yes **(B)** No

3. Dear Harvey,
   (A) Yes **(B)** No

4. Sun Valley, Idaho, 83340
   (A) Yes **(B)** No

5. Sunday, March, 20
   (A) Yes **(B)** No

6. Yours truly,
   (A) Yes **(B)** No

7. August, 7 2005
(A) Yes (B) No

8. How do I get to 391, Oak Ridge Drive?
(A) Yes (B) No

9. Football camp starts Monday, July, 25.
(A) Yes (B) No

10. We are located at 8204 Lexington Avenue, Syracuse, New York.
(A) Yes (B) No

11. Respectfully,
(A) Yes (B) No

12. Durant, Oklahoma 74701
(A) Yes (B) No

13. She walked up that hill to see more of, San Francisco California.
(A) Yes (B) No

14. The deadline is Friday, May 13.
(A) Yes (B) No

15. Dear, Aunt Rose,
(A) Yes (B) No

16. Monroe, Louisiana
(A) Yes (B) No

17. Mr. Walters moved to 259 Walnut, Street.
(A) Yes (B) No

18. Alexandria, Minnesota is not far from many lakes.
(A) Yes (B) No

19. His appointment is on Tuesday, June 14.
(A) Yes (B) No

Unit 5
Commas

- A comma sets apart words in a series of three or more items.
  Greta**,** Diego**,** and Lyla all have grandparents who live in town.
- Use a comma to separate two or more adjectives that describe the same thing if the adjective can be switched.
  The shy**,** hesitant cat stretched out its paw.
- When two complete thoughts are connected by the conjunctions *and, but,* or *or,* place a comma before the conjunction.
  Kendra unwrapped the gift**,** <u>but</u> she did not tear the bow.
  Someone opened the gate**,** <u>or</u> the wind blew it open.

Which sentence uses commas correctly?

20. **(A)** The boys went to the fair and they had a good, time.
(B) The boys went to the fair, and they had a good time.
(C) The boys went to the fair and, they had a good time.

---

21. **(A)** This festival offers food, dancing, and workshops.
(B) This festival offers food dancing, and workshops.
(C) This festival offers food, dancing and workshops.

---

22. **(A)** The sight of the golden, chilled pudding made us hungry.
(B) The sight of the, golden chilled pudding made us hungry.
(C) The sight of the golden chilled, pudding made us hungry.

---

23. **(A)** The sun was shining but, I still felt cold.
(B) The sun was shining but I still, felt cold.
(C) The sun was shining, but I still felt cold.

---

24. **(A)** Where are my keys, hat and wallet?
(B) Where are my keys, hat, and, wallet?
(C) Where are my keys, hat, and wallet?

---

25. **(A)** Dad drove the car, or, it is in the shop.
(B) Dad drove the car, or it is in the shop.
(C) Dad, drove the car or it is in the shop.

---

26. **(A)** Is that poem by Poe, Blake, or Wordsworth?
(B) Is that poem by Poe, Blake, or, Wordsworth?
(C) Is that poem by Poe, Blake or Wordsworth?

Unit 5
Commas

27. **(A)** Dust settled on the floors, windowsills, and, walls.
(B) Dust settled on the floors, windowsills and walls.
(C) Dust settled on the floors, windowsills, and walls.

28. **(A)** You can ride your bike, or, you can walk.
(B) You can ride your bike, or you can walk.
(C) You can ride your bike or, you can walk.

29. **(A)** Ken Amy and, Savita ride the same bus.
(B) Ken, Amy and Savita ride the same bus.
(C) Ken, Amy, and Savita ride the same bus.

30. **(A)** There was just enough flour, sugar, eggs, and corn oil to bake.
(B) There was just enough flour, sugar, eggs and corn oil to bake.
(C) There was just enough flour, sugar eggs, and corn oil to bake.

31. **(A)** Most people cannot resist a cute, playful, puppy.
(B) Most people cannot resist a cute, playful puppy.
(C) Most people cannot resist a cute playful, puppy.

32. **(A)** There were coupons advertisements, and notices on the board.
(B) There were coupons, advertisements, and notices on the board.
(C) There were coupons, advertisements and, notices on the board.

33. **(A)** I would have called sooner, but I woke up late.
(B) I would have called sooner, but, I woke up late.
(C) I would have called sooner but, I woke up late.

34. **(A)** Do you have a soft, fluffy, pillow?
(B) Do you have a soft fluffy, pillow?
(C) Do you have a soft, fluffy pillow?

35. **(A)** Our uncle made homemade, pretzels and we each ate one.
(B) Our uncle made homemade pretzels, and we each ate one.
(C) Our uncle made homemade pretzels and, we each ate one.

Unit 5
Commas

- Use a comma to set off the name of a person or persons being addressed.

  I do not know, Ned. Choir members, please stand on stage.
- Use a comma to set off an interjection from the rest of a sentence.

  Oh, I lost my bus pass.
- Use a comma to set off short interrupters in a sentence.

  Ellie, however, is unable to attend.
- Use a comma to separate the exact words of a speaker from the words that identify the speaker.

  Sandra asked, "Is the soup hot?" "The soup is just right," I said.
- If the speaker is identified in the middle of a sentence, put a comma before the identification within the quotation mark. Then put another comma after the identification.

  "The soup is tasty," I said, "so you should taste some."

Book Talk

Which sentence uses commas correctly?

36. **(A)** "Kent did you finish, that book last night?"
(B) "Kent, did you finish that book last night?"
(C) "Kent did you finish that book, last night?"

---

37. **(A)** "Well I, almost made it to the end."
(B) "Well, I, almost made it to the end."
(C) "Well, I almost made it to the end."

---

38. **(A)** "Oh I, should tell you the book's ending."
(B) "Oh, I should tell you the book's ending."
(C) "Oh, I, should tell you the book's ending."

---

39. **(A)** "I, however, would like to finish on my own."
(B) "I, however would like to finish on my own."
(C) "I however, would like to finish on my own."

---

40. **(A)** "Hey I will read the rest, after I finish my lunch."
(B) "Hey I, will read the rest after I finish my lunch."
(C) "Hey, I will read the rest after I finish my lunch."

Unit 5
Commas

41. **(A)** "Please do not tell me how the book ends, Justin."
(B) "Please do, not tell me how the book ends, Justin."
(C) "Please do not tell me how the book, ends Justin."

---

42. **(A)** "I will not do that," replied Justin.
(B) "I will not do that", replied Justin.
(C) "I will not do that" replied, Justin.

---

43. **(A)** Kent, asked "Am I going to like the ending?"
(B) Kent asked, "Am I going to like the ending?"
(C) Kent asked ", Am I going to like the ending?"

---

44. **(A)** "Oh, I, think so."
(B) "Oh I, think so."
(C) "Oh, I think so."

---

45. **(A)** "I wonder," said Kent "what happens to the abandoned ship."
(B) "I wonder," said Kent, "what happens to the abandoned ship."
(C) "I wonder" said Kent, "what happens to the abandoned ship."

---

46. **(A)** Justin, however, just shrugged his shoulders.
(B) Justin, however just shrugged his shoulders.
(C) Justin however, just shrugged his shoulders.

---

47. **(A)** Justin, asked "Did you look at Molly's drawing of the ship?"
(B) Justin, asked, "Did you look at Molly's drawing of the ship?"
(C) Justin asked, "Did you look at Molly's drawing of the ship?"

---

48. **(A)** "No," Kent said "I would have been late for class if I looked."
(B) "No," Kent said, "I would have been late for class if I looked."
(C) "No" Kent said, "I would have been late for class if I looked."

---

49. **(A)** "By the way," Kent, asked, "will her drawing spoil the ending?"
(B) "By the way," Kent asked, "will her drawing spoil the ending?"
(C) "By the way," Kent asked "will her drawing spoil the ending?"

---

50. **(A)** "Well, I do not think Molly's drawing will spoil the ending."
(B) "Well, I, do not think Molly's drawing will spoil the ending."
(C) "Well I, do not think Molly's drawing will spoil the ending."

Unit 6

Commas

Remember that a comma separates or sets apart specific words.

- Place a comma after an introductory word in a sentence.

  Eventually, we painted all of the rooms in our home.

  Frozen, the strawberries were placed in the sink to thaw.

  Therefore, Stan could not have mailed the letter today.

- When a sentence begins with a phrase, put a comma at the end of the phrase. Often such phrases tell where, when, or how. Remember that phrases are not complete sentences and cannot stand alone.

  From the top of the hill, I could see for miles.

  At that moment, we were all very nervous.

  Glancing at his watch, he shook his head with worry.

Track Practice

Read each passage. Look carefully at the underlined parts. Does each underlined part use commas correctly? If it does, choose *Correct*. If not, choose the answer that uses commas correctly.

(1) On, Saturday morning the team met near the field. Dew was still on the grass. Our coach blew her whistle. (2) First we did, stretches. (3) Afterward, we warmed up with several slow laps around the track.

1. **(A)** On Saturday morning the team,
   (B) On Saturday, morning the team
   (C) On Saturday morning, the team
   (D) Correct

2. **(A)** First, we, did
   (B) First, we did
   (C) First we, did
   (D) Correct

3. **(A)** Afterward we, warmed up
   (B) Afterward we warmed up,
   (C) Afterward, we, warmed up
   (D) Correct

(4) Though we stopped frequently for water, our break was an hour later. Most of us stretched on the grass. **(5)** However some stayed, in motion. **(6)** A few, minutes later Coach asked us to return. **(7)** From, her clipboard she read our workout routine. **(8)** Focused we, repeated the list to her. **(9)** Imagining, the finish line, we ran eagerly.

4. **(A)** Though, we stopped frequently for water
   (B) Though we stopped frequently, for water
   (C) Though we, stopped frequently for water
   (D) Correct

5. **(A)** However, some stayed
   (B) However, some, stayed
   (C) However some, stayed
   (D) Correct

6. **(A)** A few minutes, later Coach
   (B) A few minutes later Coach,
   (C) A few minutes later, Coach
   (D) Correct

7. **(A)** From her clipboard she read,
   (B) From, her clipboard, she read
   (C) From her clipboard, she read
   (D) Correct

8. **(A)** Focused, we repeated the list,
   (B) Focused, we repeated the list
   (C) Focused, we, repeated the list
   (D) Correct

9. **(A)** Imagining the finish line,
   (B) Imagining the finish line
   (C) Imagining the finish, line
   (D) Correct

Unit 6
Commas

- Set off an appositive phrase with commas. An appositive phrase describes a noun.

  Charlotte, the star of the play, had her costume fittings last.

  I passed by room 207, my old fourth-grade classroom.

- Set off an adverb or an adjective clause with commas. Adverb clauses describe verbs. Adjective clauses describe nouns or pronouns.

  Adverb: After we met, we sat down to talk about our assignment.

  Adjective: The assignment, which is difficult, challenges us.

Anticipation

Which sentence uses commas correctly?

10. **(A)** All I can think about is the race, which is, two days away.
(B) All I can think about is the race, which is two days away.
(C) All I can think about is the race which, is two days away.

11. **(A)** Although I was at dinner I thought of myself, winning the race.
(B) Although, I was at dinner I thought of myself winning the race.
(C) Although I was at dinner, I thought of myself winning the race.

12. **(A)** When I tried I heard, Coach's words of encouragement.
(B) When I tried, I heard Coach's words of encouragement.
(C) When I tried, I heard Coach's words, of encouragement.

13. **(A)** Coach, a former Olympian, motivates her athletes positively.
(B) Coach a former Olympian, motivates her athletes positively.
(C) Coach, a former Olympian motivates her athletes positively.

14. **(A)** Her attitude, which I admire, is that everyone who tries wins.
(B) Her attitude which, I admire, is that everyone who tries wins.
(C) Her attitude which I admire, is that everyone who tries wins.

15. **(A)** Mr. Smith our coach's, assistant, reinforces that motto.
(B) Mr. Smith our, coach's assistant, reinforces that motto.
(C) Mr. Smith, our coach's assistant, reinforces that motto.

Unit 6
Commas

16. **(A)** Though I feel stiff, I think today will be a good running day.
(B) Though, I feel stiff I think today will be a good running day.
(C) Though I feel stiff, I think, today will be a good running day.

17. **(A)** I am looking forward to, practice which is after school.
(B) I am looking forward to practice, which is after school.
(C) I am looking forward to practice which, is after school.

18. **(A)** When I close, my eyes I see myself breaking the finish line banner.
(B) When I close my eyes, I see, myself breaking the finish line banner.
(C) When I close my eyes, I see myself breaking the finish line banner.

19. **(A)** Hannah, my teammate waves, from down the hall.
(B) Hannah, my teammate, waves from down the hall.
(C) Hannah, my teammate waves from down the hall.

20. **(A)** She does her champion dance, which lets me know, she is thinking about the race too.
(B) She does her champion dance, which lets me know she is thinking about the race too.
(C) She does her champion dance which lets me know, she is thinking about the race too.

21. **(A)** While I waited for the bus, I practiced pacing my breath.
(B) While I waited, for the bus I practiced pacing my breath.
(C) While, I waited for the bus I practiced pacing my breath.

22. **(A)** Walsh Street, my bus stop is where I will start to run home.
(B) Walsh Street my bus stop, is where I will start to run home.
(C) Walsh Street, my bus stop, is where I will start to run home.

23. **(A)** Whenever, I run I will be prepared.
(B) Whenever I run, I will be prepared.
(C) Whenever I run I will, be prepared.

Unit 6
Commas

The Race

Read each passage. Look carefully at the underlined parts. Does each underlined part use commas correctly? If it does, choose *Correct*. If not, choose the answer that uses commas correctly.

(24) Finally, the day of the race arrived. (25) Even though we were, nervous we were thrilled to be there. (26) The sky which was clear, and blue, made me feel cheerful. (27) As we jogged around the track, we focused on our goals for the day. No one needed a reminder. (28) In, the spirit of, competition we were all winners.

24. **(A)** Finally, the day, of
(B) Finally the day, of
(C) Finally the day of,
(D) Correct

---

25. **(A)** Even though, we were nervous we
(B) Even though we were nervous, we
(C) Even though we, were nervous we
(D) Correct

---

26. **(A)** sky, which was clear, and blue made me
(B) sky which was clear and blue, made me
(C) sky, which was clear and blue, made me
(D) Correct

---

27. **(A)** As we jogged, around the track we focused
(B) As we jogged, around the track, we focused
(C) As we jogged around, the track we focused
(D) Correct

---

28. **(A)** In the spirit of competition, we were
(B) In the spirit, of competition we were
(C) In the spirit of competition we, were
(D) Correct

Unit 6
Commas

(29) The runners for the <u>first race, which started at 10:00 were</u> called to the line. **(30)** <u>As I lined up with the other runners spectators,</u> watching the track got quiet. **(31)** <u>Squeezing, my eyes shut, I imagined</u> the finish line. The whistle blew. **(32)** <u>Suddenly, I felt myself running</u> as fast as I could. **(33)** <u>The crowd which was, cheering loudly, became</u> a blur as I ran. **(34)** <u>Because, I tried hard I felt</u> like a winner already.

29. **(A)** first race which started at 10:00, were
(B) first race, which started at 10:00 were,
(C) first race, which started at 10:00, were
(D) Correct

---

30. **(A)** As I lined up, with the other runners spectators
(B) As I lined up with the other runners, spectators
(C) As I lined up, with the other runners, spectators
(D) Correct

---

31. **(A)** Squeezing my eyes shut, I imagined
(B) Squeezing my eyes, shut I imagined
(C) Squeezing my eyes shut I, imagined
(D) Correct

---

32. **(A)** Suddenly, I felt, myself running
(B) Suddenly I felt myself running,
(C) Suddenly I felt, myself running
(D) Correct

---

33. **(A)** The crowd, which was cheering loudly, became
(B) The crowd, which was cheering, loudly became
(C) The crowd which was cheering loudly, became
(D) Correct

---

34. **(A)** Because, I tried hard, I felt
(B) Because I tried hard, I felt
(C) Because I tried hard I, felt
(D) Correct

The Second LAP

Language Activity Pages

A. Exercising Your Skill

You have been learning about the use of abbreviations and commas. Number your paper from 1 to 12. Read the sentences below. Use a word from the box only once to complete each sentence correctly.

closing	Commas	phrases	months	one	Abbreviations
series	dictionary	before	periods	friendly	envelopes

1. A sentence that ends with an abbreviation has only _____ period.
2. _____ are a short way to write a word or a phrase.
3. Not all _____ of the year are abbreviated.
4. Street, road, and highway abbreviations are used only on _____.
5. Not all abbreviations are written with _____.
6. If you do not know a state's abbreviation, you can check a _____.
7. _____ are used to separate items in writing.
8. In _____ letters, place a comma after the greeting.
9. In all letters, place a comma after the _____.
10. Words in a _____ are three or more items.
11. In a sentence, commas are placed _____ a conjunction.
12. Different types of _____ are set off by commas.

B. Expanding Your Skill

Think of the various abbreviation rules you have learned. Number your paper from 1 to 10. Write **A, B,** or **C** on your paper to choose the abbreviation that is written correctly.

1.	**(A)** 11:59 P.M.	**(B)** 11:59 PM	**(C)** 11:59 PM.
2.	**(A)** OCT. 18	**(B)** Oct 18	**(C)** Oct. 18
3.	**(A)** Audrey C. Simms	**(B)** Audrey c. Simms	**(C)** Audrey C Simms
4.	**(A)** MON., May 9	**(B)** Mon., May 9	**(C)** Mon, May 9
5.	**(A)** 3 mL	**(B)** 3 ML	**(C)** 3 mL.
6.	**(A)** Lakeland DR	**(B)** Lakeland Dr	**(C)** Lakeland Dr.
7.	**(A)** 1 secs.	**(B)** 1 secs	**(C)** 1 sec.
8.	**(A)** MR. Petroz	**(B)** Mr. Petroz	**(C)** MR Petroz
9.	**(A)** 50 yd.	**(B)** 50 yds.	**(C)** 50 Yds.
10.	**(A)** 5 Mm	**(B)** 5 mm	**(C)** 5 mm.

C. Exploring Language

Personal Writing Number your paper from 1 to 8. Read the letter below. Each numbered part has a comma error, which could be a missing comma or a comma that is in the wrong place. If a comma is missing, write just the word that comes before it, and then write the comma. If a comma is in the wrong place, write the word that *should* come before it, and then write the comma.

Daniel Carowski
1713 Fifth Street
(1) Peru Illinois, 61354

(2) Tuesday August 2, 2005

(3) Dear, Dan

(4) Our trip to Seattle Washington, has been great! **(5)** Aside from visiting the downtown, area we have done many things related to nature. Have you ever seen a volcano? **(6)** On, Saturday we went to Mount St. Helens. **(7)** It is, however an inactive volcano that erupted in 1980 because of an earthquake. I will see you soon!

(8) Your friend
Ray

D. Expressing Yourself

Choose one of these activities. When you are finished, give your paper to your teacher.

1. Write a brief friendly letter to someone you do not get to see very often. In the letter, share what you have been doing lately, what plans you have coming up, and any special news you may have. If needed, follow the format of the letter in Part C. You can even make up a fake address if you do not know the person's real address. Use commas and abbreviations correctly in your letter.
2. **WORK with a PARTNER** With a partner, make a calendar for the current month. Do *not* abbreviate the name of the month, but use the correct abbreviations for the days of the week. On the calendar, list classmate birthdays, special class events, assignment due dates, and any other important class or school information. Use correct abbreviations when possible. Go around the classroom to ask for birthdays if necessary.

Unit 7

Colons, Semicolons, and Hyphens

A **colon** (:) and a **semicolon** (;) are punctuation marks with different purposes.

- Use a colon to separate the hour and minutes in the time of day.

  8**:**10 A.M. 2**:**35 P.M.

- Use a colon to introduce a list.

  Please bring the following items**:** pencils, paper, and clipboard.

- Use a colon after the greeting of a business letter.

  Dear Sir**:** To Whom It May Concern**:**

- Use a semicolon to join the two main clauses of a compound sentence.

  The rain had finally stopped**;** we welcomed a few rays of sun.

Miss Caldwell's Interview

Read the letter. Look carefully at the underlined parts. Does each underlined part use colons or semicolons correctly? If it does, choose *Correct*. If not, choose the answer that uses them correctly.

April 11, 2005

(1) Dear Miss Caldwell

This letter is to confirm the arrangements that have been made for your interview on Friday, April 22, 2005.

A representative from our staff will meet you at Gate C pending (2) your 9:04 A.M. flight arrival. Your first meeting is (3) scheduled for: 1015 A.M. with Mr. Dean Nelson of Human Resources. (4) Please have these items prepared: references, portfolio, and health forms. As the day continues, you will meet with (5) the following: staff members

- Miss Kay Goldman, Marketing Manager
- Mr. Louis Stilson, Director of Communications
- Mrs. Beth Spano, Advertising Coordinator

Dinner will follow with reservations (6) for 6:00 P.M. (7) We look forward to meeting you your; qualifications are impressive. If you have any questions, please do not hesitate to contact me.

Cordially,
Nina Kendall, Director of Human Resources

Unit 7
Colons, Semicolons, and Hyphens

1. **(A)** Dear: Miss Caldwell
   (B) Dear Miss: Caldwell
   (C) Dear Miss Caldwell:
   (D) Correct

2. **(A)** your: 9:04 A.M. flight
   (B) your: 904 A.M. flight
   (C) your 9:04 A.M. flight:
   (D) Correct

3. **(A)** scheduled for 1:015 A.M.
   (B) scheduled for 10:15 A.M.
   (C) scheduled for 101:5 A.M.
   (D) Correct

4. **(A)** have these items prepared references:
   (B) have: these items prepared references
   (C) have these: items prepared references
   (D) Correct

5. **(A)** the following staff members:
   (B) the: following staff members
   (C) the following staff: members
   (D) Correct

6. **(A)** for: 600 P.M.
   (B) for: 6:00 P.M.
   (C) for 60:0 P.M.
   (D) Correct

7. **(A)** forward to meeting; you your qualifications are impressive
   (B) forward to meeting you; your qualifications are impressive
   (C) forward to; meeting you your qualifications are impressive
   (D) Correct

Unit 7

Colons, Semicolons, and Hyphens

A **hyphen** (-) is another type of punctuation mark.

- Use a hyphen in numbers that are spelled out.

  I have a cousin who will be twenty-three tomorrow.

- Use a hyphen between words that show fractions and act as adjectives. The word *half,* which is a fraction, does not use a hyphen.

  one-quarter cup — The job is two-thirds complete.

- Use a hyphen in some compound words that express relationships.

  This is a photograph of my great-grandmother.

- Use a hyphen to connect two modifiers that work together.

  The ever-present stress made the job more difficult.

  I am a fifth-grade student at Edison Elementary.

- Use a hyphen between a word's syllables when you have to separate it at the end of a line of text.

  After much discussion, the Board accepted the founder's resig-
  nation with regret.

Miss Caldwell's Notes

Read Tara Caldwell's notes. Look carefully at the underlined parts. Does each underlined part use hyphens correctly? If it does, choose *Correct.* If not, choose the answer that uses hyphens correctly.

Interview Preparation — April 14, 2005

- Take large portfolio with **(8)** <u>all thirty one of my-designs</u>
- Gather **(9)** <u>work-related references and medical information</u>
- Highlight **(10)** <u>that two thirds of my college-coursework</u> was in art
- Make sure they understand that I am very serious **(11)** <u>and moti-vated about</u> this career
- Mention that my parents **(12)** <u>and great grand-father worked</u> in advertising
- Assure them that I can **(13)** <u>create thought provoking-designs</u>
- Convince them that **(14)** <u>a-high-energy environment is right for me</u>

8. **(A)** all thirty one-of-my designs
   (B) all thirty-one of my designs
   (C) all-thirty one of my designs
   (D) Correct

---

9. **(A)** work-related-references and medical information
   (B) work related references and medical-information
   (C) work related references-and-medical information
   (D) Correct

---

10. **(A)** that two-thirds-of-my college coursework
    (B) that two thirds of my-college-coursework
    (C) that two-thirds of my college coursework
    (D) Correct

---

11. **(A)** and mot-
    ivated about
    (B) and motiv-
    ated about
    (C) and motivate-
    d about
    (D) Correct

---

12. **(A)** and great-grandfather worked
    (B) and great-grand-father worked
    (C) and great grand-fath-er worked
    (D) Correct

---

13. **(A)** create thought-provoking designs
    (B) create thought-provoking-designs
    (C) create-thought provoking designs
    (D) Correct

---

14. **(A)** a-high-energy-environment is right for me
    (B) a high-energy environment is right for me
    (C) a high-energy-environment is right for me
    (D) Correct

Unit 7

Colons, Semicolons, and Hyphens

The Business Trip

Which sentence uses a colon, a semicolon, or a hyphen correctly?

15. **(A)** Tara Caldwell's flight was late there; was a delay in Denver.
(B) Tara Caldwell's flight; was late there was a delay in Denver.
(C) Tara Caldwell's flight was late; there was a delay in Denver.

---

16. **(A)** Her plane did not land until 9:38 A.M.
(B) Her plane did not land until 93:8 A.M.
(C) Her plane did not land until: 938 A.M.

---

17. **(A)** Tara's luggage could not be found on-the-ever-revolving luggage rack.
(B) Tara's luggage could not be found on the ever-revolving-luggage rack.
(C) Tara's luggage could not be found on the ever-revolving luggage rack.

---

18. **(A)** Tara claimed the following: lost items one suitcase, one briefcase, and one garment bag.
(B) Tara claimed the following lost items: one suitcase, one briefcase, and one garment bag.
(C) Tara claimed: the following lost items one suitcase, one briefcase, and one garment bag.

---

19. **(A)** Luckily, Tara held her portfolio with all thirty-one designs.
(B) Luckily, Tara held her portfolio with all-thirty one designs.
(C) Luckily, Tara held her portfolio with all thirty-one-designs.

---

20. **(A)** Tara saw a man with her name; on a sign she was relieved.
(B) Tara saw a man; with her name on a sign she was relieved.
(C) Tara saw a man with her name on a sign; she was relieved.

---

21. **(A)** Dean Nelson spent forty-five-minutes with Tara.
(B) Dean Nelson spent forty-five minutes with Tara.
(C) Dean Nelson spent forty five-minutes with Tara.

Unit 7
Colons, Semicolons, and Hyphens

The Interview

22. **(A)** Nina Kendall was out; of the office her home needed repair.
(B) Nina Kendall was out of the office; her home needed repair.
(C) Nina Kendall was out of; the office her home needed repair.

---

23. **(A)** Kay Goldman was one-quarter of an hour late meeting Tara.
(B) Kay Goldman was one quarter of-an-hour late meeting Tara.
(C) Kay Goldman was one-quarter of an hour late-meeting Tara.

---

24. **(A)** Louis Stilson focused on asking Tara about her exper-
ience.
(B) Louis Stilson focused on asking Tara about her experi-
ence.
(C) Louis Stilson focused on asking Tara about her experie-
nce.

---

25. **(A)** Beth Spano was very interested; in Tara she asked several questions about her portfolio.
(B) Beth Spano was very interested in Tara she asked; several questions about her portfolio.
(C) Beth Spano was very interested in Tara; she asked several questions about her portfolio.

---

26. **(A)** Tara is only three quarters sure she will accept the job-offer.
(B) Tara is only three quarters-sure she will accept the job offer.
(C) Tara is only three-quarters sure she will accept the job offer.

---

27. **(A)** These are Tara's worries company: size, moving, and stability.
(B) These are Tara's: worries company size, moving, and stability.
(C) These are Tara's worries: company size, moving, and stability.

---

28. **(A)** Staff members who met Tara consider her a top-quality candidate.
(B) Staff members who met Tara consider her a top quality-candidate.
(C) Staff members-who-met Tara consider her a top quality candidate.

Unit 8

Quotation Marks and Underlining

Quotation marks (" ") are another type of punctuation mark.

- Quotation marks enclose certain titles, including stories, articles, songs, poems, and book chapters.

  The sport headline reads **"**Harper Squeaks by Central.**"**

  The eighth chapter is named **"**Lost and Found.**"**

Note that the end mark goes within the closing quotation mark, even if it is not part of the title.

- Quotation marks enclose the exact words of a speaker.

  "Has anyone seen Andy?**"** asked Mr. Matthews.

  Zach said, **"**Andy missed the bus this morning.**"**

If the speaker is identified in the middle of a sentence, use two sets of quotation marks. Remember that the end mark goes within the closing quotation mark.

  "Andy's aunt,**"** Zach continued, **"**will probably drive him here.**"**

- Quotation marks do *not* enclose indirect speech.

  Zach explained that Andy's aunt and uncle are his neighbors.

Today's Topic

Which sentence uses quotation marks correctly?

1. **(A)** "Is everyone ready to share something by his or her favorite author? asked Mrs. Loomis."
   (B) Is everyone ready to share something by his or her favorite author? "asked Mrs. Loomis."
   (C) "Is everyone ready to share something by his or her favorite author?" asked Mrs. Loomis.

2. **(A)** "Paolo," she requested, "please move that chair to the center."
   (B) "Paolo, "she requested," please move that chair to the center."
   (C) "Paolo, she requested, please move that chair to the center."

3. **(A)** Paolo went first; the poem he read was "Tundra Sky".
   (B) Paolo went first; the poem he read was "Tundra Sky.
   (C) Paolo went first; the poem he read was "Tundra Sky."

4. (A) Erik chose to read a passage from "The Celebrated Jumping Frog of Calaveras County by Mark Twain."
(B) Erik chose to read a passage from "The Celebrated Jumping Frog of Calaveras County" by Mark Twain.
(C) Erik chose to read a passage from The Celebrated Jumping Frog of Calaveras County by "Mark Twain."

5. (A) "Mrs. Loomis said, I enjoy reading Mark Twain's stories as well."
(B) Mrs. Loomis said, "I enjoy reading Mark Twain's stories as well".
(C) Mrs. Loomis said, "I enjoy reading Mark Twain's stories as well."

6. (A) "Who knows Mark Twain's real name?" asked Mrs. Loomis.
(B) "Who knows Mark Twain's real name? asked Mrs. Loomis."
(C) "Who knows Mark Twain's real name"? asked Mrs. Loomis.

7. (A) "His real name," commented Andrea, "was Samuel Clemens."
(B) "His real name, commented Andrea, was Samuel Clemens."
(C) "His real name, "commented Andrea, was Samuel Clemens."

8. (A) "Andrea, said Mrs. Loomis, "please share your selection next."
(B) "Andrea," said Mrs. Loomis, "please share your selection next."
(C) "Andrea," said Mrs. Loomis, please share your selection next."

9. (A) She sat in the designated chair to read the article "Trees for Life."
(B) She sat in the designated chair to read the article "Trees for Life".
(C) She sat in the designated chair to read "the article Trees for Life."

10. (A) "Jasmine chose a song; the song's title was I Hope You Dream."
(B) Jasmine chose a song; the song's title was "I Hope You Dream."
(C) "Jasmine chose a song;" the song's title was I Hope You Dream.

11. (A) "Thank you all, "concluded Mrs. Loomis," for sharing today."
(B) "Thank you all, concluded Mrs. Loomis, for sharing today."
(C) "Thank you all," concluded Mrs. Loomis, "for sharing today."

Unit 8

Quotation Marks and Underlining

Underline the titles of books, magazines, plays, newspapers, movies, and works of art when you write. In print, titles are usually italicized.

Book: Hop on Pop is fun to read.

Magazine: Cobblestone is a good history magazine.

Play: The drama department is rehearsing The Miracle Worker.

Newspaper: Do you get The Plain Dealer?

Movie: Was The Little Princess in black and white?

Art: This painting is called Ship in a Storm.

An italicized title ⟶ *Hop on Pop*

Media Mania

Which sentence uses underlining correctly?

12. **(A)** This library always has the most current Gazette.
    (B) This library always has the most current Gazette.
    (C) This library always has the most current Gazette.

---

13. **(A)** Lorna found a copy of the book A Wrinkle in Time.
    (B) Lorna found a copy of the book A Wrinkle in Time.
    (C) Lorna found a copy of the book A Wrinkle in Time.

---

14. **(A)** Hailey looked for a magazine called Collector's Collectibles.
    (B) Hailey looked for a magazine called Collector's Collectibles.
    (C) Hailey looked for a magazine called Collector's Collectibles.

---

15. **(A)** On the wall, there was a new poster of a beautiful statue named Winged Victory of Samothrace.
    (B) On the wall, there was a new poster of a beautiful statue named Winged Victory of Samothrace.
    (C) On the wall, there was a new poster of a beautiful statue named Winged Victory of Samothrace.

---

16. **(A)** Treasure Island has already been checked out at this location.
    (B) Treasure Island has already been checked out at this location.
    (C) Treasure Island has already been checked out at this location.

17. **(A)** The oversized books area had a book called Art of the <u>Louvre</u>.
(B) The oversized books area had a book called <u>Art of the Louvre</u>.
(C) The <u>oversized books</u> area had a book called Art of the Louvre.

---

18. **(A)** The <u>Louvre</u> is a museum in Paris, France; one of its most well-known works of art is the Mona Lisa.
(B) The Louvre is a museum in <u>Paris, France</u>; one of its most well-known works of art is the Mona Lisa.
(C) The Louvre is a museum in Paris, France; one of its most well-known works of art is the <u>Mona Lisa</u>.

---

19. **(A)** Moving toward the magazines, I saw <u>an issue</u> of Science Quarterly.
(B) Moving toward the magazines, I saw <u>an issue of Science Quarterly</u>.
(C) Moving toward the magazines, I saw an issue of <u>Science Quarterly</u>.

---

20. **(A)** It was an issue I had already read, so I picked up a copy of <u>National Geographic Kids</u>.
(B) It was an issue I had already read, so I picked up a copy of National <u>Geographic Kids</u>.
(C) It was an issue I had already read, so I picked up a copy of National Geographic <u>Kids</u>.

---

21. **(A)** Two of the articles I read reminded me of story ideas I had for our <u>school newspaper</u>, The Cavalier.
(B) Two of the articles I read reminded me of story ideas I had for our school newspaper, <u>The Cavalier</u>.
(C) Two of the articles I read reminded me of <u>story ideas</u> I had for our school newspaper, The Cavalier.

---

22. **(A)** There was also a book review in the magazine that recommended Black Beauty, <u>a novel</u> about a horse.
(B) There was also a book review in the magazine that recommended <u>Black Beauty, a novel</u> about a horse.
(C) There was also a book review in the magazine that recommended <u>Black Beauty</u>, a novel about a horse.

Unit 8
Quotation Marks and Underlining

Library News

Read each passage. Look carefully at the numbered parts. Does each numbered part use quotation marks or underlining correctly? If it does, choose *Correct*. If not, choose the answer that does.

The librarian said, **(23)** "This area will be helpful as you begin your history projects." Our local Historical Society has published **(24)** a volume of poetry called Early <u>American</u> Poems. It includes some poems written by children, **(25)** such as "My Sod House". **(26)** The latest issue of <u>Discover</u> magazine is a great resource for our projects. **(27)** The article 10 Great "Events in American" History might provide alternative project ideas.

23. **(A)** "This area will be helpful" as you "begin your history projects."
(B) This area will be helpful "as you begin your history projects."
(C) "This area will be helpful as you begin your history projects".
(D) Correct

---

24. **(A)** a volume of poetry called <u>Early American</u> Poems.
(B) a volume of poetry called <u>Early American Poems</u>.
(C) a volume of poetry called Early <u>American Poems</u>.
(D) Correct

---

25. **(A)** such as "My Sod House"
(B) "such as "My Sod House."
(C) such as "My Sod House."
(D) Correct

---

26. **(A)** The latest issue of <u>Discover magazine</u>
(B) The <u>latest issue</u> of Discover magazine
(C) The latest <u>issue of Discover</u> magazine
(D) Correct

---

27. **(A)** The article "10 Great Events in American History"
(B) The article "10 Great Events" in American History
(C) The article 10 Great Events in "American History"
(D) Correct

Unit 8

Quotation Marks and Underlining

(28) "In addition, explained the librarian, here are other resources about the War of 1812 and the Civil War." We have a film, which is **(29)** also a documentary, entitled Off to War. The film **(30)** incorporates soldiers' songs, such as "Lincoln and Liberty." One student asked the librarian, **(31)** How do I know if a source is reliable or not?" The librarian referred the student to an article, **(32)** "Ready Resources", to explain the process of selecting dependable sources.

28. **(A)** "In addition," explained the librarian, here are other resources about the War of 1812 and the Civil War."
(B) "In addition, explained the librarian, "here are other resources about the War of 1812 and the Civil War."
(C) "In addition," explained the librarian, "here are other resources about the War of 1812 and the Civil War."
(D) Correct

---

29. **(A)** also a documentary, entitled Off to War
(B) also a documentary, entitled Off to War
(C) also a documentary, entitled Off to War
(D) Correct

---

30. **(A)** incorporates soldiers' songs, such as "Lincoln and "Liberty."
(B) incorporates soldiers' songs, such as "Lincoln and Liberty".
(C) incorporates soldiers' songs, such as "Lincoln and Liberty"
(D) Correct

---

31. **(A)** "How do I know if a source is reliable or not"
(B) "How do I know if a source is reliable or not?"
(C) "How do I know if a source is reliable or not"?
(D) Correct

---

32. **(A)** "Ready Resources," to explain the process
(B) "Ready Resources, to explain the process
(C) Ready Resources," to explain the process
(D) Correct

The Third LAP
Language Activity Pages

A. Exercising Your Skill

You have been learning about a variety of punctuation marks and when to underline words and phrases. Number your paper from 1 to 12. Read each sentence below to decide if it is true or false. If the sentence is true, write the letter **T** on your paper. If the sentence is false, then write the letter **F** on your paper.

1. A semicolon separates the hour and minutes in the time of day.
2. A colon can introduce things in a list.
3. A hyphen is an example of an end mark.
4. Book titles are set off by quotation marks.
5. The titles of plays and works of art are underlined.
6. A hyphen is used in numbers that are spelled out in writing.
7. A semicolon can be used to join two main clauses.
8. Quotation marks set off the exact words of a speaker.
9. An end mark is placed outside of a closing quotation mark.
10. Newspaper titles are set off by underlining.
11. Colons should not be used after the greeting of a business letter.
12. Hyphens are never used in compound words.

B. Expanding Your Skill

Think of the hyphen rules you have learned. Number your paper from 1 to 12. The sentences below are all missing hyphens. On your paper, write the words from each sentence correctly with hyphens.

1. Where is bus fifty nine?
2. I am nearly twenty five minutes late for my meeting.
3. I hope they understand my transportation related excuse.
4. I cannot control the traffic, which occurs three fourths of the time.
5. At the meeting, many people were forty five minutes late.
6. It seems that the day started out poorly for at least two thirds of us.
7. My sister in law kept track of the meeting's topics and minutes.
8. She is a well trained secretary; she is very skilled in shorthand.
9. She told me about the meeting at a party for my great grandmother.
10. Sadly, less than one quarter of the family could attend the party.
11. The meeting actually ended thirty five minutes early.
12. We thought we might avoid what seems like ever present traffic.

C. Exploring Language

Poetry Number your paper from 1 to 5. Read the poem about punctuation marks below. You will notice that some of the poem's words are missing. Fill in each blank with a punctuation rule you have learned. The rules you choose should make sense, and some rhyme with the last word in the line before it.

My business letter has been stolen,
and I forgot to use a _____.
Now its greeting is alone.
I know I wrote main clauses.
I think they were compound,
but my _____ is nowhere to be found.
I ran into Mr. Q. Marks to ask him a question,
But he said, "You're silly, I'm Mr. _____."
A word I left hang-
ing was looking for its _____.
Now it'll never know
where it's supposed to go.
I hope the last sentence is going to be fine,
I wrote so many titles but with no _____.

D. Expressing Yourself

Choose one of these activities. When you are finished, give your paper to your teacher.

1. Find an article in a newspaper or a magazine. On your paper, write the article's title. If the article is long, use only the first three paragraphs. Look for colons, hyphens, and quotation marks. Recall the rules you have learned. For each of these punctuation marks in the article, write the rule it follows. For example, if you find a colon in a time of day, write the word *time* on your paper. If you find a hyphen in a number that is spelled out, write *number*. Or, if you find a book chapter in quotation marks, write *chapter*. There are other rules you may have to name on your own.
2. **WORK with a PARTNER** With a partner, think of a company you would like to start together. Write a short business letter to a bank asking for a loan to start the company. When necessary, correctly use punctuation marks you have learned. Be sure to include details about the company.

Unit 9

Dashes, Parentheses, Ellipses Points, and Apostrophes

There are two types of **dashes.** A **long dash** (—) is sometimes used in place of commas to set off ideas that need emphasis.

Those guests were rowdy—but there is no need to discuss them.

Talk with your partner—quietly—about ideas for your essay.

A **short dash** (–), which is longer than and different from a hyphen, is used to separate spans of numbers, such as scores, years, and ages.

The score is 20–3. Units 5–9 1875–1975 6:00 A.M.–8:00 A.M.

- Use **parentheses** ( ) to enclose information that explains or to set off extra information, such as definitions, in a sentence. The sentence should be able to stand alone *without* the material in parentheses.

Charles Dickens (1812–1870) wrote *The Pickwick Papers*.

The deposition (testimony in court) has been recorded.

Note that a comma falls after and outside of parentheses. A sentence's punctuation should not appear within parentheses.

Which sentence uses dashes or parentheses correctly?

1. **(A)** The band room you know where that is—is where we meet.
(B) The band room—you know where that is—is where we meet.
(C) The band—room you know where that is—is where we meet.

2. **(A)** Someone told me (based on the condition) of not being named that the deal is now complete.
(B) Someone told me (based on the condition of) not being named that the deal is now complete.
(C) Someone told me (based on the condition of not being named) that the deal is now complete.

3. **(A)** Based on the schedule (sent home yesterday), our next deadline is Friday.
(B) Based on the schedule (sent home yesterday,) our next deadline is Friday.
(C) Based on (the schedule sent home yesterday), our next deadline is Friday.

4. **(A)** Chapters 31–34 will be covered on tomorrow's exam.
(B) Chapters–31–34 will be covered on tomorrow's exam.
(C) Chapters–31–34–will be covered on tomorrow's exam.

5. **(A)** Dad removes—gently and carefully his oatmeal cookies from the tray.
   (B) Dad removes—gently and carefully—his oatmeal cookies from the tray.
   (C) Dad removes gently and carefully—his oatmeal cookies from the tray.

---

6. **(A)** As the mountains erode (see Diagram 2-1,) the appearance of the landscape changes dramatically.
   (B) As the mountains erode (see Diagram 2-1), the appearance of the landscape changes dramatically.
   (C) As the mountains (erode see Diagram 2-1), the appearance of the landscape changes dramatically.

---

7. **(A)** The show was great—you would not believe the skill of the dancers!
   (B) The show was great you would not believe—the skill of the dancers!
   (C) The show was—great you would not believe the skill of the dancers!

---

8. **(A)** Harry S. Truman 1884–1972 was the thirty-third president of the United States from (1945 until 1953).
   (B) Harry S. Truman 1884–1972 was (the thirty-third president) of the United States from 1945 until 1953.
   (C) Harry S. Truman (1884–1972) was the thirty-third president of the United States from 1945 until 1953.

---

9. **(A)** My flight—leaving from Iowa—was fine, yet a little bumpy.
   (B) My flight—leaving from Iowa was fine, yet a little bumpy.
   (C) My—flight leaving from Iowa was—fine, yet a little bumpy.

---

10. **(A)** This particular fjord (the Norwegian word for “a narrow bay of water between cliffs or steep slopes” was a breathtaking sight.
    (B) This particular fjord (the Norwegian word for) “a narrow bay of water between cliffs or steep slopes” was a breathtaking sight.
    (C) This particular fjord (the Norwegian word for “a narrow bay of water between cliffs or steep slopes”) was a breathtaking sight.

Unit 9

Dashes, Parentheses, Ellipses Points, and Apostrophes

Ellipses points (. . .) are three periods spaced apart equally. They are used to show that part of a quotation has been left out. Like other punctuation, ellipses points should be within the quotation marks.

Cicero wrote, "**. . .** Either write things worth reading or do things worth the writing."

Churchill said, "Come on now, all you young men, **. . .** accept your responsibilities."

An **apostrophe** (') takes the place of one or more letters left out of a contraction.

does not → doesn**'**t they will → they**'**ll

she would → she**'**d you are → you**'**re

- Apostrophes are used in possessive nouns but *not* possessive pronouns.

  The dog is Kelly's. → The dog is hers. (*not* her's)

- Do not use an apostrophe to form the plural of a family name.

  The Tuckers are on vacation. (*not* Tuckers' or Tucker's)

Which sentence is punctuated correctly?

11. **(A)** That boy said this basketball is his'.
(B) That boy said this basketball is his.
(C) That boy said this basketball is his's.

---

12. **(A)** A philosopher, Jean-Jacques Rousseau, wrote, "However great a man's natural talent .. the act of writing cannot be learned all at once."
(B) A philosopher, Jean-Jacques Rousseau, wrote, "However great a man's natural talent . . . . . . the act of writing cannot be learned all at once."
(C) A philosopher, Jean-Jacques Rousseau, wrote, "However great a man's natural talent . . . the act of writing cannot be learned all at once."

---

13. **(A)** Harold doesn't know if he will be at the party on time.
(B) Harold does'not know if he will be at the party on time.
(C) Harold doesnt' know if he will be at the party on time.

14. **(A)** "And so, my fellow Americans," said President John F. Kennedy, ". . . Ask what you can do for your country."
(B) "And so, my fellow Americans," said President John F. Kennedy, . . . "Ask what you can do for your country."
(C) . . . "And so, my fellow Americans," said President John F. Kennedy, ". . . Ask what you can do for your country."

---

15. **(A)** Your neighbor asked us if the truck parked in the driveway was our's.
(B) Your neighbor asked us if the truck parked in the driveway was ours.
(C) Your neighbor asked us if the truck parked in the driveway was ours'.

---

16. **(A)** Do you know that the Tapman's are moving to Boston?
(B) Do you know that the Tapmans' are moving to Boston?
(C) Do you know that the Tapmans are moving to Boston?

---

17. **(A)** We're hoping to visit Hawaii on our next vacation.
(B) Wer'e hoping to visit Hawaii on our next vacation.
(C) Were' hoping to visit Hawaii on our next vacation.

---

18. **(A)** Author C. S. Lewis. . . stated, "No book is really worth reading at the age of ten which is not equally. . . worth reading at the age of fifty and beyond."
(B) Author C. S. Lewis stated, "No book is really worth reading at the age of ten which is not equally . . . worth reading at the age of fifty and beyond."
(C) Author C. S. Lewis stated, . . ."No book is really worth reading at the age of ten which is not equally worth reading at the age of fifty and beyond."

---

19. **(A)** I think you've given me the wrong assignment, because we have yet to study the Ottoman Empire.
(B) I think yo'uve given me the wrong assignment, because we have yet to study the Ottoman Empire.
(C) I think youv'e given me the wrong assignment, because we have yet to study the Ottoman Empire.

Unit 9

Dashes, Parentheses, Ellipses Points, and Apostrophes

Which sentence uses dashes, parentheses, ellipses points, and apostrophes correctly?

20. **(A)** I will send that file (from last week once) I have reviewed it.
(B) I will send that file (from last week once I) have reviewed it.
(C) I will send that file (from last week) once I have reviewed it.

---

21. **(A)** Did he read pages 7–15?
(B) Did he read pages–7–15?
(C) Did he read pages 7–15–?

---

22. **(A)** "Friends, Romans, Countrymen . . ." is the beginning to a well-recognized speech from history.
(B) "Friends, Romans, Countrymen . . ." . . . is the beginning to a well-recognized speech from history.
(C) "Friends, Romans, Countrymen" . . . is the beginning to a well-recognized speech from history.

---

23. **(A)** Devin hopes shel'l get a part in the ballet.
(B) Devin hopes she'll get a part in the ballet.
(C) Devin hopes sh'ell get a part in the ballet.

---

24. **(A)** Hand me—your clay—projects slowly as you leave the classroom today.
(B) Hand me your clay projects—slowly—as you leave the classroom today.
(C) Hand me your clay projects slowly as—you leave—the classroom today.

---

25. **(A)** William (Randolph) Hearst 1863–1951 published newspapers.
(B) William Randolph Hearst (1863–1951 published) newspapers.
(C) William Randolph Hearst (1863–1951) published newspapers.

---

26. **(A)** Marcus wondered if the coat on the hanger was yours.
(B) Marcus wondered if the coat on the hanger was your's.
(C) Marcus wondered if the coat on the hanger was yours'.

Unit 9

Dashes, Parentheses, Ellipses Points, and Apostrophes

27. **(A)** A (wallaby) an animal in the kangaroo family eats plants.
(B) A wallaby (an animal in the kangaroo family) eats plants.
(C) A wallaby an animal in the kangaroo (family eats plants).

28. **(A)** The Berger's enjoy going to the high school's sporting events.
(B) The Bergers enjoy going to the high schools sporting events.
(C) The Bergers enjoy going to the high school's sporting events.

29. **(A)** I think it was Picasso who said, . . . A painting is a dramatic action in the course of which reality finds itself split apart.
(B) I think it was Picasso who said, . . . "A painting is a dramatic action in the course of which reality finds itself split apart."
(C) I think it was Picasso who said, ". . . A painting is a dramatic action in the course of which reality finds itself split apart."

30. **(A)** The legend of Amelia Earhart (1897-1937) is based partly on her mysterious disappearance.
(B) The legend of (Amelia Earhart) 1897-1937 is based partly on her mysterious disappearance.
(C) The legend of Amelia Earhart—1897-1937—is based partly on her mysterious disappearance.

31. **(A)** Those landscapers—though not from this area—have many customers in our neighborhood.
(B) Those landscapers—though not from this area have many customers in our neighborhood.
(C) Those—landscapers—though not from this area have many customers in our neighborhood.

32. **(A)** Scheduled from (11:00 A.M.-3:00 P.M.,) orientation includes lunch.
(B) Scheduled from 11:00 A.M.-3:00 P.M., orientation includes lunch.
(C) Scheduled from-11:00 A.M.-3:00 P.M., orientation includes lunch.

Unit 10

Capitalization and Punctuation

Exercises in this unit review some capitalization and punctuation skills.

What Begins with a Capital Letter?

- First word in a sentence
- The pronoun *I*
- Pet names
- People's names, initials, and titles
- Words used as names
- First word of a quotation or a speaker
- Historical periods
- Holidays, languages, religions, and nationalities
- Cities, counties, states, countries, and continents
- Bodies of water and geographical places
- Special events
- Days, months, greetings, and first word of a letter's closing
- Main words in titles, documents, awards, and structures
- Most product names, businesses, and abbreviations

In which part of each sentence is there a capitalization error? If there is *not* an error, choose *None*.

1. Is my brother (A) | howie in (B) | your class? (C) | None (D)

2. We are (A) | currently studying (B) | the Renaissance. (C) | None (D)

3. The mma (A) | does not have (B) | Renaissance resources. (C) | None (D)

4. MMA stands (A) | for the Museum of (B) | Modern Art. (C) | None (D)

5. The renaissance (A) | is not a (B) | modern movement. (C) | None (D)

6. The Renaissance (A) | had its beginnings (B) | in italy. (C) | None (D)

7. It spread through (A) | europe between (B) | the 14th and 17th centuries. (C) | None (D)

8. Renaissance itself (A) | can be defined as (B) | "a rebirth or revival." (C) | None (D)

Unit 10
Capitalization and Punctuation

Where Would I Go?

9.	This writing	assignment is something	i cannot wait to write!	None
	(A)	(B)	(C)	(D)
10.	Our teacher,	mrs. frantz, asked us	to think of faraway places.	None
	(A)	(B)	(C)	(D)
11.	We would imagine	spending all of July	in one faraway place.	None
	(A)	(B)	(C)	(D)
12.	we would list	what to take, such as food,	clothes, and music.	None
	(A)	(B)	(C)	(D)
13.	My first thought	was to look for	an island near australia.	None
	(A)	(B)	(C)	(D)
14.	My next thought	was to look at	a map of the mediterranean.	None
	(A)	(B)	(C)	(D)
15.	Then i decided	that one month on an island	is too long.	None
	(A)	(B)	(C)	(D)
16.	Finally I chose	egypt as the topic	of my assignment.	None
	(A)	(B)	(C)	(D)
17.	Exploring egypt's history,	I felt that I would	not be bored.	None
	(A)	(B)	(C)	(D)
18.	Water is near	enough to that location	of northeast africa.	None
	(A)	(B)	(C)	(D)
19.	There are two bordering	seas: the Mediterranean	and the Red.	None
	(A)	(B)	(C)	(D)
20.	Of course, there	is also the massive	nile river in Egypt.	None
	(A)	(B)	(C)	(D)

Unit 10
Capitalization and Punctuation

Here are some punctuation rules from previous units.
- Sentences that tell or command end with a period.
- Periods are used in many abbreviations.
- Questions end with a question mark. Sentences that show strong feeling end with an exclamation point.
- Commas are used in dates and certain words or phrases.
- Colons introduce lists. Semicolons can separate main clauses.
- Hyphens are used in some numbers and compound words.

Read each letter. Look carefully at the underlined parts. Is each underlined part punctuated correctly? If it is, choose *Correct.* If not, choose the answer that is punctuated correctly.

(21) <u>Wednesday November 16, 2005</u>

Dear Superintendent Maxwell,

In last month's newsletter, (22) <u>you wrote about the new lunch plan</u> (23) <u>I am a fifth-grader at Hastings.</u> I have used the plan for a few weeks; I think it works well. Now those who buy lunch do not worry about bringing money to school. It is like we have a lunch credit card.

(24) <u>Thank you</u>
Simon Burwell

21. **(A)** Wednesday, November 16 2005
    (B) Wednesday, November 16, 2005
    (C) Wednesday, November, 16 2005
    (D) Correct

22. **(A)** you wrote about the new lunch plan.
    (B) you wrote about the new lunch plan!
    (C) you wrote about the new lunch plan?
    (D) Correct

23. **(A)** I am a fifth grader at Hastings.
    (B) I am a-fifth-grader at Hastings.
    (C) I am a fifth grader-at-Hastings.
    (D) Correct

24. **(A)** Thank you:
    (B) Thank you;
    (C) Thank you,
    (D) Correct

Unit 10
Capitalization and Punctuation

Monday, November 21, 2005

Dear Simon,

Thank you for your letter. **(25)** Twenty one other students wrote to me about the lunch plan. Many students wrote that they sometimes forget **(26)** their lunch cards; some of them wondered if they could just memorize the ID number. I explained how easy it would be for incorrect accounts to be charged. **(27)** If lunch cards were not seen, it would also be too easy for a dishonest student to use a different number? I hope students will understand because I value your input. In the future, **(28)** here are other ways to: share your ideas student council meetings, e-mail, comment cards, and the school's Web site.

Sincerely,
Superintendent Maxwell

25. **(A)** Twenty-one other students wrote to me
(B) Twenty-one-other-students wrote to me
(C) Twenty-one-other students wrote to me
(D) Correct

26. **(A)** their lunch cards, some of them wondered
(B) their lunch cards some of them wondered;
(C) their lunch cards: some of them wondered
(D) Correct

27. **(A)** If lunch cards, were not seen it would also be too easy for a dishonest student to use a different number?
(B) If lunch cards were, not seen it would also be too easy for a dishonest student to use a different number!
(C) If lunch cards were not seen, it would also be too easy for a dishonest student to use a different number.
(D) Correct

28. **(A)** here are other ways to share your ideas: student council meetings, e-mail, comment cards, and the school's Web site.
(B) here are other ways to share your ideas; student council meetings, e-mail, comment cards, and the school's Web site.
(C) here are other ways: to share your ideas student council meetings, e-mail, comment cards, and the school's Web site.
(D) Correct

The Last LAP
Language Activity Pages

A. Exercising Your Skill

You have been learning about long and short dashes, parentheses, ellipsis points, and apostrophes. You have also had the chance to review some capitalization and other punctuation skills. Number your paper from 1 to 12. Read each sentence below to decide if it is true or false. If the sentence is true, write the letter **T** on your paper. If the sentence is false, then write the letter **F** on your paper.

1. Short dashes can be used in place of commas.
2. Short dashes are used to separate spans of numbers, including scores and units in books.
3. A short dash is shorter than a hyphen.
4. Long dashes can be used in place of commas.
5. Long dashes set apart ideas in a sentence that need emphasis.
6. A sentence's punctuation appears outside of parentheses.
7. A sentence should not be able to stand alone without the information in parentheses.
8. An apostrophe cannot take the place of letters in a contraction.
9. An apostrophe is not used to refer to the plural of a family name.
10. Ellipsis points are made by putting three commas together.
11. Ellipsis points show that part of a quotation has been left out.
12. In writing, ellipsis points should appear within quotation marks.

B. Expanding Your Skill

Think of the apostrophe rules you have learned. Number your paper from 1 to 10. The sentences below all have a word that is missing one apostrophe. Find the words. On your paper, write each word correctly with its apostrophe.

1. It doesnt look like the store is open.
2. Theres a sign hanging in the window.
3. The stores owner or manager must have written it.
4. The sign says, "Well be back by 1:30. Sorry for the inconvenience."
5. Thats nice that he or she put a sign up for customers.
6. Id like to get lunch while we are waiting.
7. Youve always wanted to try that restaurant next door.
8. Then well be able to see when the store opens again.
9. I think thats a great idea.
10. Im hungry just talking about it.

C. Exploring Language

Descriptive Writing Number your paper from 1 to 6. Read the paragraph below. Look carefully at the underlined parts. Each underlined part is missing a short dash, long dashes, or parentheses. On your paper, write the underlined part correctly with its missing punctuation.

Enzo Ferrari

Enzo Ferrari 1898–1988 is a man you may or may not know of. If anything, you know his last name from the automobile legacy he built. Enzo born in Modena, Italy knew at a young age that he wanted cars to be a major part of his life. While working for a small carmaker, Enzo started racing cars in 1919. Though moving upward in the ranks, Enzo's racing career was in doubt from 1925 1928. Then in 1929 he started his own company. Other car enthusiasts people devoted strongly to a cause or an interest helped Enzo establish a reputation of the highest quality and workmanship. This paved the road no pun intended for Enzo to start his own racing team. So, if you ever see a Ferrari, know that it has a history of love and loyalty behind it.

D. Expressing Yourself

Choose one of these activities. When you are finished, give your paper to your teacher.

1. Think of a topic you would like to research. Get the encyclopedia volume that would have that topic in it. For example, if you chose *astronomy*, get encyclopedia Volume A. Read five paragraphs of your topic's entry in the encyclopedia. If there are not five paragraphs, you may choose another topic. Look for dashes, parentheses, ellipsis points, and apostrophes in the entry. Write down each example you find with its punctuation. Then write your own examples using what you found as a model. For example, if there was a definition in parentheses, write a definition related to your topic in parentheses.
2. WORK with a PARTNER With a partner, select something in your school that needs to be improved. Write a friendly letter to your principal about it. Be sure to include at least one suggestion about how to fix the problem or how to improve the situation. In the letter, correctly use at least one example of a short dash *or* long dashes, an apostrophe, and parentheses.

MECHANICS Scope and Sequence • *Specific Skill Series for Language Arts*

Unit/Level	Level A	Level B	Level C	Level D	Level E	Level F	Level G	Level H
Unit 1	Capital Letters	Capital Letters	Capital Letters	Capital Letters	Capitalization	Capitalization	Capitalization	Capitalization
Unit 2	Capital Letters	Capital Letters	Capital Letters	Capital Letters	Capitalization	Capitalization	Capitalization	Capitalization
Unit 3	Capital Letters	Capital Letters	Capital Letters	Capital Letters	End Marks	Capitalization	Capitalization	Capitalization
Unit 4	Capital Letters	End Marks	End Marks	End Marks	Abbreviations	End Marks	End Marks	End Marks
Unit 5	End Marks	Capital Letters and End Marks	Abbreviations	Abbreviations	Commas	Abbreviations	Quotation Marks	Abbreviations
Unit 6	End Marks	Commas	Commas	Commas	Commas	Commas	Abbreviations	Commas
Unit 7	End Marks	Commas	Commas	Commas	Colons, Semicolons, and Hyphens	Commas	Commas	Commas
Unit 8	Capital Letters and End Marks	Commas	Colons	Commas	Quotation Marks and Underlining	Commas	Commas	Commas
Unit 9	Capital Letters and End Marks	Quotation Marks	Quotation Marks	Colons	Other Punctuation Marks	Colons, Semicolons, and Hyphens	Commas	Colons, Semicolons, and Hyphens
Unit 10	Contractions and Apostrophes	Contractions and Apostrophes	Underlining	Hyphens	Capitalization and Punctuation	Quotation Marks and Underlining	Colons and Semicolons	Quotation Marks and Underlining
Unit 11		Capitalization and Punctuation	Capitalization and Punctuation	Quotation Marks and Underlining		Other Punctuation Marks	Hyphens	Other Punctuation Marks
Unit 12			Capitalization and Punctuation	Capitalization and Punctuation		Capitalization and Punctuation	Underlining	Capitalization and Punctuation
Unit 13							Other Punctuation Marks	
Unit 14							Capitalization and Punctuation	